Disaster Survivors Erased by a TORNADO!

by Jessica Rudolph

Consultant: Daphne Thompson
Meteorologist, Educational Outreach Coordinator
Cooperative Institute for Mesoscale Meteorological Studies
National Weather Center

BEARPORT
PUBLISHING

New York, New York

Credits

Cover, © Patryce Bak/Workbook Stock/Getty Images and Zastolskiy Victor Leonidovich/Shutterstock; Title Page, © Zastolskiy Victor Leonidovich/Shutterstock; 4, © Jim Veneman/Union University; 5, © Jessica Rinaldi/Reuters/Landov; 6, © Rick Gershon/Getty Images; 7, © AP Images/Andrew McMurtrie/The Jackson Sun; 8, © Matthew Diggs/Union University; 10TL, © A. T. Willett/Alamy; 10BL, © A. T. Willett/Alamy; 10R, © Sean Martin/iStockphoto; 11, © Reuters/Landov; 12, © Weatherstock/Omniphoto; 14, © Jim Reed/Severe & Unusual Weather/Corbis; 16, © Bettmann/Corbis; 17L, Courtesy of Joseph Marinaro; 17R, © Win Henderson/FEMA; 18L, © Bettmann/Corbis; 18R, © AP Images; 19, © Bettmann/Corbis; 20T, © Matthew Cavanaugh/epa/Corbis; 20C, © A. T. Willett/Alamy; 20B, © AP Images/Sue Ogrocki; 21, © AP Images/Mark Humphrey; 22L, © Jim Reed/Science Faction/Corbis; 22R, Courtesy of NOAA; 23, © Jim Reed/Severe & Unusual Weather/Corbis; 24, © Jim Reed/Severe & Unusual Weather/Corbis; 25TL, © AP Images/Clay Jackson/The Advocate Messenger; 25TR, © Weatherstock/Omniphoto; 25B, Courtesy of Midland Radio; 26T, © 2009, OPUBCO Communications Group/Paul Hellstern/The Oklahoman; 26B, © 2009, OPUBCO Communications Group/Paul Hellstern/The Oklahoman; 27, © Morris Abernathy/Union University; 28, © AP Images/Fred Stewart; 29, Courtesy of Walter Disney.

Publisher: Kenn Goin
Editorial Director: Adam Siegel
Creative Director: Spencer Brinker
Design: Dawn Beard Creative
Photo Researcher: Omni-Photo Communications, Inc.

Library of Congress Cataloging-in-Publication Data

Rudolph, Jessica.
  Erased by a tornado! / by Jessica Rudolph.
     p. cm. — (Disaster survivors)
  Includes bibliographical references and index.
  ISBN-13: 978-1-936087-52-5 (lib. bdg.)
  ISBN-10: 1-936087-52-9 (lib. bdg.)
  1. Tornadoes—United States—Juvenile literature. I. Title.
  QC955.2.R83 2010
  551.55'3—dc22
                              2009034363

For more information, write to Bearport Publishing Company, Inc., 101 Fifth Avenue, Suite 6R, New York, New York 10003. Printed in the United States of America in North Mankato, Minnesota.

122009
090309CGD

10 9 8 7 6 5 4 3 2 1

Contents

Remembering a Disaster

It was Tuesday, February 5, 2008. Mikias (mih-KEE-uhss) Mohammed (muh-HAH-mid) was doing homework in his **dorm room**. Around 7:00 P.M. he heard warning **sirens**. Students at Union University in Jackson, Tennessee, knew what the sirens meant. A **tornado** was dangerously close.

Tornadoes are columns of air that spin fiercely in a circle and stretch down from a storm cloud to the ground. Tornadoes are also called *twisters, whirlwinds,* and *cyclones.*

Union University before the tornado hit

There was no time to find shelter. The tornado was barreling down onto the school. Suddenly the lights in Mikias's room went out. Then he heard a noise that sounded like a train. "After that I couldn't hear anything—the windows shattered and the wind smashed me against the wall," remembered Mikias. "Everything just started to fall down."

Union University after the tornado hit

Surviving the Twister

After the tornado crashed its way through the university, Mikias was buried under what was once the walls and ceiling of his room. Despite being hit on the head by falling **debris**, Mikias clawed his way out of the **rubble**. Then he spotted several other students huddled together. They were covered in blood. Terrified and hurt, Mikias started screaming. The other students helped Mikias stay calm until help arrived.

Union University students look at the damage caused by the tornado.

When emergency workers found the students, Mikias was rushed to a hospital. Doctors told him he would have headaches for a while but would eventually be fine. Mikias was just one of many students who were injured in the monster storm.

Dozens of injured students were taken to the hospital after the tornado hit Jackson, Tennessee.

Most people who die in tornadoes are killed by flying debris, such as chunks of wood, brick, or glass.

A Huge Outbreak

When Mikias returned to the school, he couldn't believe his eyes. The building he had lived in was nothing but a pile of metal, bricks, and wood. Mikias is from the African country of Ethiopia. He said, "I have never experienced anything like this. We don't have this kind of weather back home."

Mikias Mohammed at Union University after it was hit by the tornado

The tornado was just one of 87 tornadoes that hit several states on Tuesday, February 5, 2008, and the next day as well. This event is known as the Super Tuesday tornado **outbreak**. Fortunately, nobody at the university died. Others were not so lucky. Tornadoes killed 57 people in Alabama, Arkansas, Kentucky, and Tennessee in those two days.

Super Tuesday Tornado Outbreak: February 5–6, 2008

Kansas
Missouri
Illinois
Indiana
Kentucky
West Virginia
Virginia
North Carolina
Oklahoma
Jackson
Tennessee
South Carolina
Arkansas
Mississippi
Georgia
Texas
Louisiana
Alabama

— Where the tornadoes hit

UNITED STATES

N
W E
S

When many tornadoes occur during a storm, it's called an *outbreak* or a *cluster*. The largest tornado outbreak happened on April 3 and 4, 1974. It included 148 tornadoes across 13 states.

Anything Can Happen

Tornadoes can be deadly because they are powerful and **unpredictable**. They usually occur in the spring or summer. Yet they can happen any time of the year. Many Super Tuesday survivors said they were caught off guard by tornadoes in February.

A twister can take many different shapes. It can be cone-shaped, wispy like smoke, or thin and ropelike. There's no way to tell how destructive a tornado will be, however, based on its shape or size.

Tornadoes are unpredictable in other ways, too. They can be less than 100 feet (30.5 m) wide or more than 2 miles (3.2 km) wide. While most tornadoes move less than 1 mile (1.6 km), some travel more than 100 miles (161 km). They can last from a few seconds to more than an hour. In June 2008, a tornado ripped quickly through a Boy Scout camp in Iowa. In less than 10 seconds, four scouts were killed.

Tornadoes can flatten buildings while leaving others nearby untouched.

Tornado Weather

How do tornadoes start? They are all born from violent thunderstorms. These powerful storms are caused when warm and cold **air masses** crash into each other.

When air masses collide, warm air rises because it is lighter than cold air. As it rises, the warm air cools down. The cooling causes **water vapor** in the air to turn into tiny water droplets. If there are enough droplets, thunderstorm clouds form.

Severe thunderstorms can have dark clouds, lightning, and hail.

Some of the strongest storms in the world form over flat land where there are no mountains to block the flow of air masses. In the **Great Plains**, for example, cool air moving south from Canada meets warm air coming north from the Gulf of Mexico. Some of the thunderstorms that form from air masses over the Great Plains create tornadoes.

Tornadoes in the United States

CANADA

WA
MT
ND
MN
OR
ID
SD
WI
WY
NE
IA
MI
VT
ME
NH
MA
NY
RI
CT
NJ
PA
OH
DE
MD
NV
UT
CO
KS
MO
IL
IN
WV
VA
CA
AZ
NM
OK
AR
KY
TN
NC
SC

UNITED STATES

TX
LA
MS
AL
GA

FL

PACIFIC OCEAN

ATLANTIC OCEAN

N
W   E
S

Gulf of Mexico

MEXICO

☐ Great Plains
☐ Tornado Alley

Most tornadoes in the world occur in the United States. Many of these happen in an area known as Tornado Alley, which is made up of part of the Great Plains and surrounding areas.

Usually, the United States has about 1,000 tornadoes every year. However, 2008 was an especially bad year, with almost 1,700 tornadoes.

13

A Spinning Giant

It's a mystery to **meteorologists** why some thunderstorms create tornadoes while most do not. Scientists do know that terrible thunderstorms have high-speed winds that move in different directions. When these winds pass over one another, they can form a sideways, or **horizontal**, tube of air below the thunderstorm.

A twister can start out invisible. It gets its dark color when it picks up dust and dirt from the ground.

When warm air near the ground shoots upward, it can push the spinning tube so that it stands straight up. If the tube spins fast enough and close to the ground, a **funnel cloud** can form. When this powerful spinning cloud touches the ground, it is called a tornado.

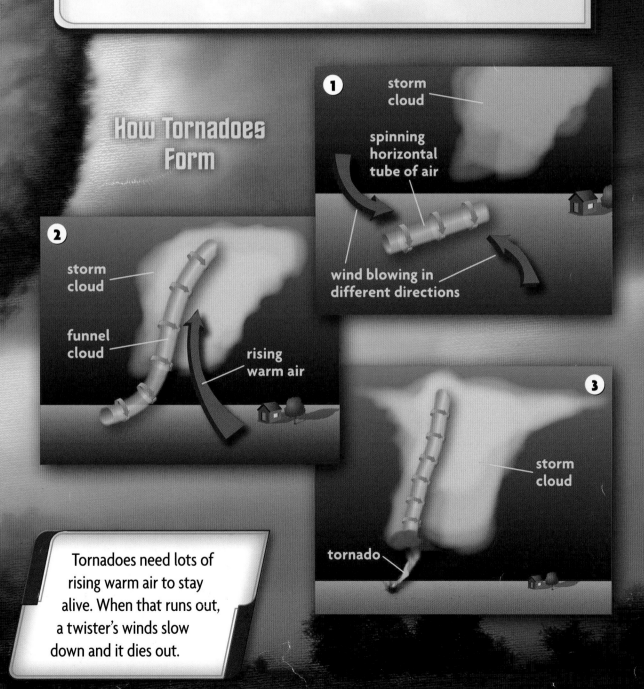

How Tornadoes Form

1
storm cloud

spinning horizontal tube of air

wind blowing in different directions

2
storm cloud

funnel cloud

rising warm air

3
storm cloud

tornado

Tornadoes need lots of rising warm air to stay alive. When that runs out, a twister's winds slow down and it dies out.

The Fastest Winds on Earth

After a tornado has formed, scientists try to measure its wind speeds. It's not very easy to do this, however. Twisters are very powerful. Most weather **instruments** placed in their paths get destroyed. In 1971, however, meteorologist Ted Fujita (foo-JEE-tuh) found a way around this problem.

Ted Fujita performed experiments to learn about tornadoes.

The winds of a tornado are the fastest on Earth—even faster than the winds of a **hurricane**.

Fujita **estimated** tornado wind speeds based on how much damage they did. His Fujita Scale ranked tornadoes from weakest (F0) to strongest (F5). Fujita estimated that F5 tornadoes had winds faster than 260 miles per hour (418 kph). Winds that strong can blow a house off its **foundation**.

Damage caused by an F1 tornado (left) and an F3 tornado (right)

Enhanced Fujita Scale

EF Scale	Wind Speed	Type of Damage
EF0	65–85 mph (105–137 kph)	Signs and chimneys damaged; branches broken off from trees; some trees pushed over
EF1	86–110 mph (138–177 kph)	Surface of roofs peeled off; mobile homes overturned; cars pushed off roads
EF2	111–135 mph (178–217 kph)	Roofs torn off houses; mobile homes destroyed; large trees snapped or ripped out of the ground
EF3	136–165 mph (218–266 kph)	Roofs and some walls torn off well-built houses; trains overturned; most trees in forests ripped out of the ground
EF4	166–200 mph (267–322 kph)	Well-built houses destroyed; structures with weak foundations blown off some distance; cars thrown
EF5	More than 200 mph (more than 322 kph)	Strong houses lifted off foundations and carried long distances; cars may fly through the air for more than 328 feet (100 m)

In 2007, meteorologists updated the Fujita Scale so that it more accurately describes the damage caused by tornadoes. Using this Enhanced Fujita Scale, scientists now rate tornadoes from EF0 to EF5.

The Deadliest Tornado

When she was 13, Gladys Whipkey lived through a horrible F5 called the Tri-State Tornado. On March 18, 1925, Gladys and her classmates were playing in their schoolyard in Illinois as the storm twisted toward them. "My mother, who was a teacher in my school, saw the tornado approach," remembered Gladys. "She rang the bell, the signal to come inside. I was upset because recess had ended so early."

This school in Murphysboro, Illinois, was completely demolished by the Tri-State Tornado.

During the Tri-State Tornado, this house in Griffin, Indiana, flew 50 feet (15 m) and landed on its side.

Gladys made it only halfway up the stairway, however, before it collapsed. Falling bricks struck her. The young girl was knocked out for hours. The twister also flattened her home. Still, Gladys survived the deadliest twister in U.S. history. The Tri-State Tornado killed 695 people in Missouri, Illinois, and Indiana.

These men searched for survivors buried under rubble after the tornado hit Griffin, Indiana.

On average, tornadoes cause about 70 deaths and 1,500 injuries in the United States every year.

Bizarre Sights

After the Tri-State Tornado, a Missouri newspaper reported that the twister had swept many things into the air—stoves, houses, even a cow! Tornadoes can make all sorts of strange things happen. They can peel roads away and pluck people off the ground.

A tornado in Virginia picked up this truck and threw it against the wall of a medical building.

This fork was flung into a tree by a tornado in Texas.

A tornado in Oklahoma twisted the top of this electrical tower.

Tornadoes have been known to suck up fish and frogs from lakes and drop them onto dry land.

In 2008, a Super Tuesday tornado in Tennessee flung 11-month-old Kyson Stowell 300 feet (91 m) from his house. Kyson's home was crushed. Amazingly, he was fine.

Paul Nelson wasn't tossed into the air when a tornado hit his Oklahoma home in 1947. Almost everything else was, though. Paul was taking a bath when the twister lifted up his house. All that was left on the ground was Paul sitting in his bathtub!

Kyson Stowell, pictured with his great-grandmother, was picked up by a tornado and thrown about the distance of a football field! Except for a few scratches, Kyson was fine.

Chasing the Storm

Since Paul Nelson's day, scientists have made many improvements in the instruments they use to predict tornadoes. Today, **radar** stations can track bad storms. These stations send out radio waves into the air. When they hit storm clouds, the waves bounce back and create an image of the storm on a computer screen. Meteorologists are then able to use this information to **forecast** tornadoes and warn people.

A radar station (above) and scientists using computers to track a storm (left)

Scientists still do not know enough about how tornadoes form to predict them far in advance. The average warning time that meteorologists can give to people in a tornado's path before it hits is 13 minutes.

Scientists called "storm chasers" also work to predict twisters. They follow thunderstorms, waiting for a tornado to form. Storm chasers have **portable** radar and other instruments in their trucks. They measure things like the air temperature and the direction of winds. That information helps them learn more about how and when twisters form.

Storm chasers in a truck studying a tornado in Kansas

Preparing for the Unexpected

The work of storm chasers may help increase warning times—and save people's lives. People who hear earlier tornado warnings on the radio or television have more time to find shelter. Storm cellars and basements are the safest places. These underground rooms guard people from shattered glass and other debris tossed around by tornadoes.

Tami Jantz took cover in her storm cellar when a tornado struck her home in Kansas.

Towns and cities can also help protect people. Some communities have tornado sirens that can be heard for miles. Many schools also hold tornado **drills**. During these drills, children practice the duck-and-cover position. In this pose, children kneel down and place their hands over their heads to shield them from flying debris.

These schoolchildren in Kentucky are practicing the duck-and-cover position during a tornado drill.

The National Oceanic and Atmospheric Administration (NOAA) sells special radios that automatically broadcast a severe weather warning as soon as it is issued.

NOAA radios (above) and tornado sirens (right) are particularly helpful at night when people are sleeping and not aware of bad weather.

Rebuilding a Community

After a tornado hits a community, the next step is rebuilding. An F5 tornado battered Oklahoma City in 1999. Many survivors decided to build underground shelters while reconstructing shattered buildings. Oklahoma City is located in Tornado Alley. There is a good chance the shelters will be needed one day.

The 1999 Oklahoma City tornado damaged or completely destroyed almost 10,000 homes and businesses. Today, the city has been rebuilt—as seen in these pictures taken in 1999 (left) and 2009 (below).

The city most likely to be struck by a tornado is Oklahoma City. Since 1893, it has been slammed by tornadoes more than 120 times!

At Union University, life moved on quickly after the 2008 Super Tuesday outbreak. Construction began a few weeks after the tornado. The buildings that were erased in the storm were replaced.

Around the same time, students returned to classes. Mikias Mohammed may have lost his belongings, but he is looking to the future. "Everything is gone, but I am thankful we all made it," he said.

Construction crews at Union University

Famous Tornadoes

Many tornadoes in U.S. history have caused a massive amount of damage and led to hundreds of deaths. Here are a few of the most famous twisters.

Natchez Tornado: May 7, 1840

- The Natchez Tornado started in Louisiana. It then moved across the Mississippi River into Natchez, Mississippi.
- The tornado flattened forests on both sides of the Mississippi River. While moving over the river, it destroyed and sunk several boats.
- The twister, which is the second-deadliest tornado in U.S. history, killed 317 people. Of those killed, 269 had been on boats.

Tri-State Tornado: March 18, 1925

- The Tri-State Tornado started in Missouri and journeyed east into Illinois and Indiana.
- The twister traveled 219 miles (352 km) in under four hours. Survivors reported that it was about one mile (1.6 km) wide.
- The Tri-State Tornado killed 695 people—the most of any tornado in U.S. history.

Super Outbreak: April 3–4, 1974

- The world's largest tornado outbreak is known as the Super Outbreak. It included 148 tornadoes that touched down in 13 states in the South and Midwest.
- All the twisters combined traveled a total of 2,500 miles (4,023 km) and killed around 330 people.
- The single tornado that caused the most deaths in the outbreak was the one that hit Xenia (ZEEN-yuh), Ohio, where nearly 35 people died. More than 1,000 people were injured. About half of the city's buildings were damaged or destroyed.

This tornado hit Xenia, Ohio, on April 3, 1974.

Tornado Safety

Here are some tornado safety tips.

☑ During a bad storm, listen for weather updates on the radio or television. A *tornado watch* means that weather conditions are bad enough for a tornado to possibly form. A *tornado warning* means that a tornado has been sighted nearby. Find shelter immediately!

☑ Keep in mind that a twister can form suddenly with no warning. Just before a tornado hits, the sky may have a greenish color, there may be hail or a large, dark cloud, or you may hear a loud sound similar to a speeding train. Any of these signs means you should rush to take cover.

☑ The safest place to be during a tornado is a basement or a storm cellar. If you're in a house or other building with no underground shelter, go to the ground floor. Try to find a small space with no windows, such as a bathroom or hallway. Place a mattress or heavy blanket over your head to protect yourself from falling debris.

☑ It is not safe to be in a car during a tornado. Instead, get out and find shelter in a sturdy building. If there isn't one nearby, run outside and lie in a ditch with your hands over your head. Stay away from trees, which can fall on top of you.

TORNADO SHELTER

Places such as shopping centers may have signs like this one to show people where they can take shelter during a tornado.

Glossary

air masses (AIR MASS-iz) bodies of air that cover huge areas

debris (duh-BREE) the parts of something that was broken or destroyed

dorm room (DORM ROOM) short for dormitory room; a room that is used by a college student for studying and sleeping

drills (DRILZ) plans of action that are practiced over and over

estimated (ESS-ti-*mayt*-id) to have figured out the approximate amount of something

forecast (FOR-kast) to predict

foundation (foun-DAY-shuhn) a base made of stone, concrete, or other material that supports a building from underneath

funnel cloud (FUHN-uhl KLOUD) a spinning tube of air that hangs down from a storm cloud; if it touches the ground, it becomes a tornado

Great Plains (GRAYT PLAYNZ) the grasslands in North America that cover much of the central United States and parts of Canada

horizontal (hor-uh-ZON-tuhl) flat; level with the ground

hurricane (HUR-uh-*kayn*) a powerful storm with heavy rains and fast winds that forms over a large body of water such as an ocean or sea

instruments (IN-struh-muhnts) scientific tools used to record or measure something

meteorologists (*mee*-tee-ur-OL-oh-jists) scientists who study the weather

outbreak (OUT-brayk) a sudden increase in the activity of something

portable (POR-tuh-buhl) easy to move

radar (RAY-dar) a tool that can find the location of an object by sending out radio waves

rubble (RUHB-uhl) a pile of broken things

sirens (SYE-ruhnz) warning devices that make loud, piercing sounds

tornado (tor-NAY-doh) a violent, whirling column of air that moves over the land and can cause much destruction

unpredictable (*uhn*-pri-DIK-tuh-buhl) not able to be known ahead of time

water vapor (WAW-tur VAY-pur) water in the form of a gas

Bibliography

Burt, Christopher C. *Extreme Weather: A Guide and Record Book.* New York: W. W. Norton (2007).

Cerveny, Randy. *Freaks of the Storm: From Flying Cows to Stealing Thunder, the World's Strangest True Weather Stories.* New York: Thunder's Mouth Press (2006).

Coppock, Mike. "The Devil in the Night." *American History* (April 2007), pp. 54–59.

www.spc.noaa.gov/faq/tornado/

Read More

Ball, Jacqueline A. *Tornado! The 1974 Super Outbreak (X-treme Disasters That Changed America).* New York: Bearport Publishing (2005).

Berger, Melvin and Gilda. *Do Tornadoes Really Twist? Questions and Answers About Tornadoes and Hurricanes.* New York: Scholastic (2000).

Lindop, Laurie. *Chasing Tornadoes.* Brookfield, CT: Twenty-First Century Books (2003).

Woods, Michael and Mary B. *Tornadoes.* Minneapolis, MN: Lerner (2007).

Learn More Online

To learn more about tornadoes, visit
www.bearportpublishing.com/DisasterSurvivors

Index

About the Author

Jessica Rudolph has edited many books about history, geography, and nature. She recently moved to Phoenix, where she discovered a love for hiking and spelunking.